# Duck's New

Juliette MacIver & Carla Martell

SCHOLASTIC
SYDNEY AUCKLAND NEW YORK TORONTO LONDON MEXICO CITY
NEW DELHI HONG KONG BUENOS AIRES PUERTO RICO

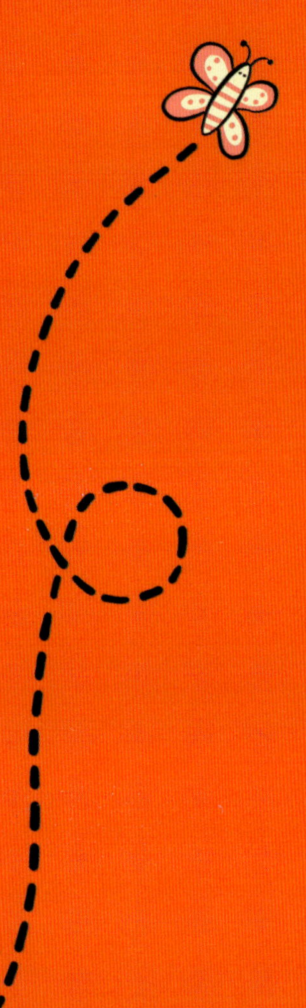

For Willow Worth, the tiny Queen of Words ~ J.M.

For Ngaio, who always loves a good story xxx ~ C.M.

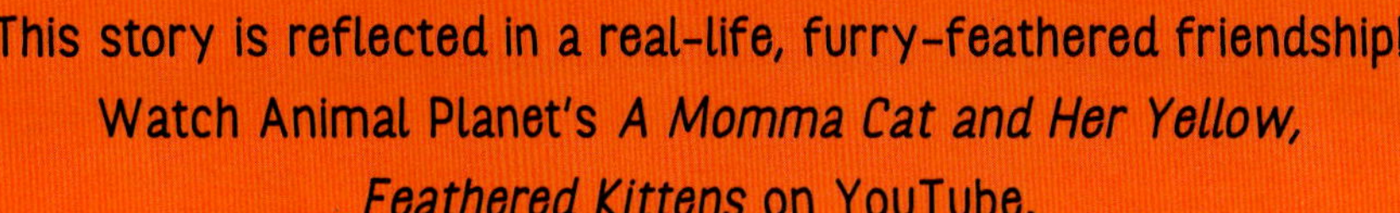

This story is reflected in a real-life, furry-feathered friendship!
Watch Animal Planet's *A Momma Cat and Her Yellow, Feathered Kittens* on YouTube.

First published in 2025 by Scholastic New Zealand Limited
Private Bag 94407, Botany, Auckland 2163, New Zealand

Scholastic Australia Pty Limited
PO Box 579, Gosford, NSW 2250, Australia



ISBN 978-1-77543-916-5



A catalogue record for this book is available from the National Library of New Zealand.

12 11 10 9 8 7 6 5 4 3 2 1 5 6 7 8 9 / 2

Publishing team: Lynette Evans, Penny Scown and Abby Haverkamp
Designer: Vida Kelly
Typeset in Shaking Three
Printed in China by RR Donnelley

Scholastic New Zealand's policy is to use papers that are renewable and made efficiently from wood grown in responsibly managed forests, so as to minimise its environmental footprint.

Duck's a duck –
and sure of that.
But Duck is also . . .

quite the cat!

Mama Cat has taught Duck how

to stalk and pounce,

and speak

meow.

One day, Duck goes
waddling off,
to see who lives
behind the trough.

says Pig.
And Duck thinks, "My!
Here's a brand new
word to try!"

So Duck puffs up
a feathered breast.

says Duck.

And Pig's impressed!

Then off goes Duck,
down roads unsealed,
to see who lives out
in the field.

says Horse.
And Duck thinks, "Hey!
Another brand new
word to say!"

So Duck breathes in.
With lungs all filled . . .

says Duck.

And Horse is thrilled!

Then Duck goes
waddling on beyond,
to see who lives out
on the pond.

It's four big ducks.
They all say

QUACK.

And Duck thinks,
"What on earth was that?!"

Duck tries.

Then

and

"A duck," they gasp,
"who cannot quack!"

A kind duck asks,
"What can you say?"
And Duck says

The ducks are really
most impressed.
"Teach us OINK
and all the rest!"

Then Pig and Horse
come down the way.
"Duck, you called!
Need help?" they say.

So Duck begins,
with Pig and Horse,
to teach
a foreign language course.

The ducks soon master

**OINK**

and

**NEIGH**

But MEOW

they cannot seem to say.

Duck can, though.
Imagine that!

Because Duck's a duck,

and . . .

quite the cat.